The Deutsche Bibliothek holds
a record for this publication in the
Deutsche Nationalbibliografie;
detailed bibliographical data can
be found under http://dnb.ddb.de

Library of Congress Control
Number is available

©2010, Foster + Partners,
London, and Prestel Verlag,
Munich · Berlin · London ·
New York

Prestel Verlag, A Member
of Verlagsgruppe Random
House GmbH

Prestel Verlag
Königinstrasse 9
80539 Munich
Germany
Tel  +49 (089) 242908-300
Fax +49 (089) 242908-355
www.prestel.de

Prestel Publishing
900 Broadway, Suite 603
New York NY 10003
USA
Tel  +1 (212) 995-2720
Fax +1 (212) 995-2733

Prestel Publishing Ltd
4 Bloomsbury Place
London
WC1A 2QA
UK
Tel  +44 (020) 7323-5004
Fax +44 (020) 7636-8004
www.prestel.com

ISBN 978-3-7913-4493-5

# Hearst Tower Foster + Partners

Norman Foster
Joseph Giovannini

**PRESTEL**
MUNICH · BERLIN · LONDON · NEW YORK

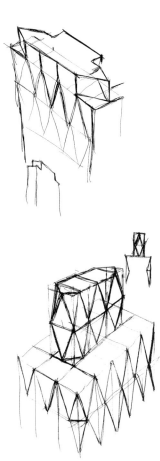

In these sketches Norman Foster explores the relationship between the base of the new tower and the existing Hearst building and alternative treatments for the top of the tower.

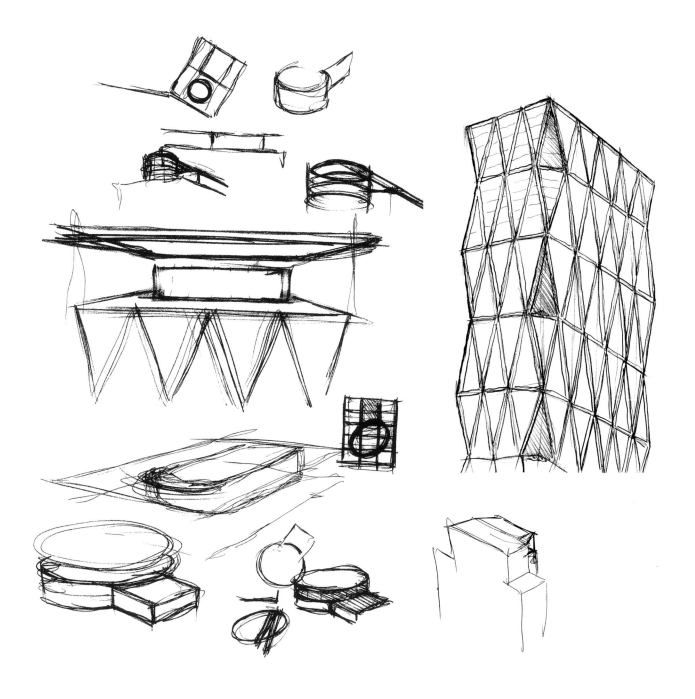

## **Introduction** Norman Foster

Hearst Tower revives a dream from the 1920s, when the publishing magnate William Randolph Hearst envisaged Columbus Circle as the hub of a new media quarter in Manhattan. As a base for his growing US newspaper and magazine empire, Hearst commissioned a building for a site at 959 Eighth Avenue, which he ambitiously named the International Magazine Building. His architect for the six-storey block was Joseph Urban, an Austrian émigré – and originally a set designer – with a reputation for idiosyncrasy, something you see demonstrated on Eighth Avenue. Urban was teamed with George B Post & Sons, a New York firm renowned for the design of office buildings.

Hearst and his architects anticipated that the building on Eighth Avenue would eventually form the base of a nine-storey tower, though so far as we know, no such scheme was ever drawn. The challenge for us, in designing a tower at some seventy years remove, was to find a way of creating a dialogue between a contemporary structure and a base that was highly unusual in its expression, to the extent that it enjoyed New York City Landmark status.

Since 1928, when the Eighth Avenue building was completed, the world and the Hearst organisation have changed dramatically. The pace of change is such that the way people work today is quite different from even ten years ago. Great strides in technological innovation in all areas including communications media, publishing and architecture have made designing in this new century all the more enthralling. How then to produce a building that would allow Hearst to bring together 2,000 employees in one location; that would be capable of responding to change in coming decades; that would attract and hold the best workforce in an increasingly competitive market; that would be distinctive in its own right; and would communicate the values of the Hearst Corporation and maintain its pre-eminence as an organisation for the foreseeable future?

Added to that, how to create a presence on the New York skyline that would represent optimism and a sign of good things to come after the trauma of the city's recent history? I was in Manhattan for a meeting with Hearst on 11 September 2001 when the two aircraft struck the World Trade Center towers. That act dealt a potential body blow to the future of high-rise building in the city – at one moment you could almost feel the city's confidence slipping away. However, in deciding to move forward with the project so soon after 9/11, Hearst sent a conscious message to the world that the business community in New York remained positive about the city's future as a place to work and thrive and that as a company it was ready to invest in Manhattan.

Immediately following 9/11 – and quite independently – we brought together a multidisciplinary team with structural engineers, vertical transportation consultants and fire experts working alongside architects to conduct in-depth research into the optimal design of tall buildings. We wanted to ensure that, should such a terrible event ever be repeated, structural failure and disastrous loss of life would not follow. We gained a huge amount of knowledge from that exercise and many of those lessons informed the design of Hearst Tower.

I believe that from Hearst's point of view, a crucial factor in our gaining the commission was our work in the context of historic structures – in projects as diverse as the Reichstag in Berlin and the Royal Academy of Arts in London and the Great Court at the British Museum, in London. Usually in the context of a historic building – a parliament building or a great museum – where the layers of history are complex and intertwined, one's instinct as an architect is to establish a respectful relationship between old and new, but one nonetheless in which each has its own clearly articulated voice.

However, in the context of an office building – one that had really reached the end of its working life – we sensed that there was an opportunity to be bold.

While the shell of Urban's building had to be conserved, our studies quickly led us to the conclusion that nothing within those walls could sensibly be retained. Then, by scooping out the existing fabric and moving all the offices to the upper floors, we saw that the entire shell of the historic base could be recast to create a generous lobby on the scale of a piazza – an 'urban room' that would mediate between the building's private spaces and the public realm and form the social heart of the Hearst community.

The lobby occupies the entire floor plate of the old building and rises up through six floors at its highest point. Like a bustling town square, this space provides access to all parts of the building. It incorporates the main elevator lobby, the Hearst staff restaurant – Café 57 – the Joseph Urban Theater and mezzanine spaces for meetings, exhibitions and special functions. It is contained by the original windowed masonry walls, which echo the tone and texture of the Art Deco exterior. If the tower is about expressing the office in the city, then the lobby seeks to bring the city into the office.

As we developed the design of the lobby, we realised the opportunity to work with two quite different but complementary artists. The first of these collaborations was with the glass specialist James Carpenter and Jim Garland of Fluidity in the creation of 'Icefall'. A major feature of the lobby is the series of diagonal escalators that provide a connection with street level. The escalators rise through a two-storey cascade of chilled water, which plays a significant environmental role, reusing rainwater collected from the roof to cool the lobby in summer and humidify the space in winter.

James Carpenter's intervention has given the waterfall a further dimension. By devising a system of cast-glass prisms that capture and refract light, he has made the cascading water sparkle with sunlight, just as it would in nature.

Richard Long brought nature inside the building in another sense, with RIVERLINES – a wall piece set against the grey stone of the elevator core. Like a cave painting for the twenty-first century, it is made from mud harvested from the banks of the Avon and Hudson rivers and celebrates the metaphor of the river as a symbol of journey, movement and life.

Working with artists in this way is an experience that is both pleasurable and informative. For however strong an image of a space you hold in your mind or however well you think you know it, an artist can help you to see it with fresh eyes. Appropriately, RIVERLINES is both monumental yet incredibly quiet. It is a commanding presence, yet it invites closer inspection – in fact the closer you get the more you see.

Stand on the floor of the lobby and look up and you become aware of another presence. The forty-four-storey tower rises above you, linked to the walls of the old building by a skirt of glazing that encourages an impression of the tower floating weightlessly above the base. Structurally, the tower has a diagrid form – a very efficient, lightweight triangulated solution which has its roots in the pioneering work of Buckminster Fuller and structural innovators such as Barnes Wallis. In the context of Hearst, the diagrid meant that we needed 20 per cent less steel than we would have done if we had adopted a conventionally framed structure. Added to that, 85 per cent of the steel we used came from recycled sources, so it was doubly efficient.

The diagrid also works at the urban scale, establishing a distinctive profile on the skyline. We decided to peel back the corners of the tower between the diagonals in a series of open 'birds' mouths' which have the effect of emphasising the building's vertical proportions. Uniquely, from inside the offices, the cutaway corners reveal diagonal views across the Midtown Manhattan grid. The tower does not have a conventional New York flourish on top – its crystalline form is cut straight – but it literally sparkles, its form and colour shifting with the changing light and cast of the weather.

As a company, Hearst places a high value on the quality of the working environment – something it believes will become increasingly important to its staff in the future. We worked with Hearst to create a building that is highly significant in terms of its sustainable credentials, one that not only consumes far less energy than a conventional high-rise office building, but also provides a working environment that is light-filled and naturally ventilated, utilising outside air ventilation for up to 75 per cent of the year.

To put that achievement into perspective, the building is designed to consume 25 per cent less energy than it would had we complied minimally with New York State and City codes. As a result, it was the first office building in Manhattan to apply for, and be awarded, a gold rating under the US Green Building Council's Leadership in Energy and Environmental Design (LEED) programme.

In that sense, it has been a groundbreaking project for the city. When we first began talking to Hearst in 2001, the conventional wisdom among developers was that sustainable design was too expensive for Manhattan – it ate into the bottom line. However, by looking at the lifetime costs of the building, we were able to demonstrate that the reality was very different. Efficiencies in construction and over the building's life cycle more than offset the initial 'green' premium. We could show that, for a company with a long-term interest in occupying the building, there was a strong business incentive to invest in sustainable design.

Interestingly, that experience reinforces a long-held conviction that it is the owner-occupiers – companies such as Willis Faber, the Hongkong and Shanghai Bank and Commerzbank – who are the real drivers of innovation in office building design. As they set the bar higher, so the commercial market follows. If that pattern is repeated, Hearst Tower may well prove to be the herald in Manhattan of a new generation of sustainable buildings to come.

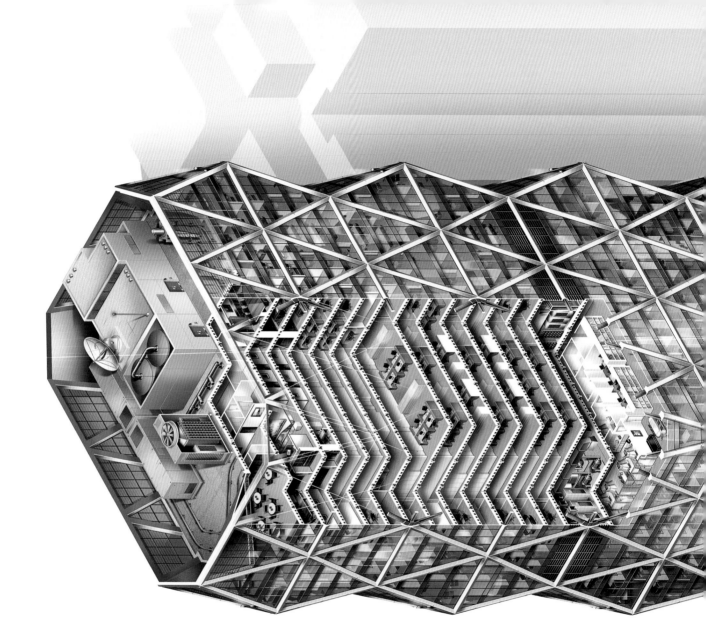

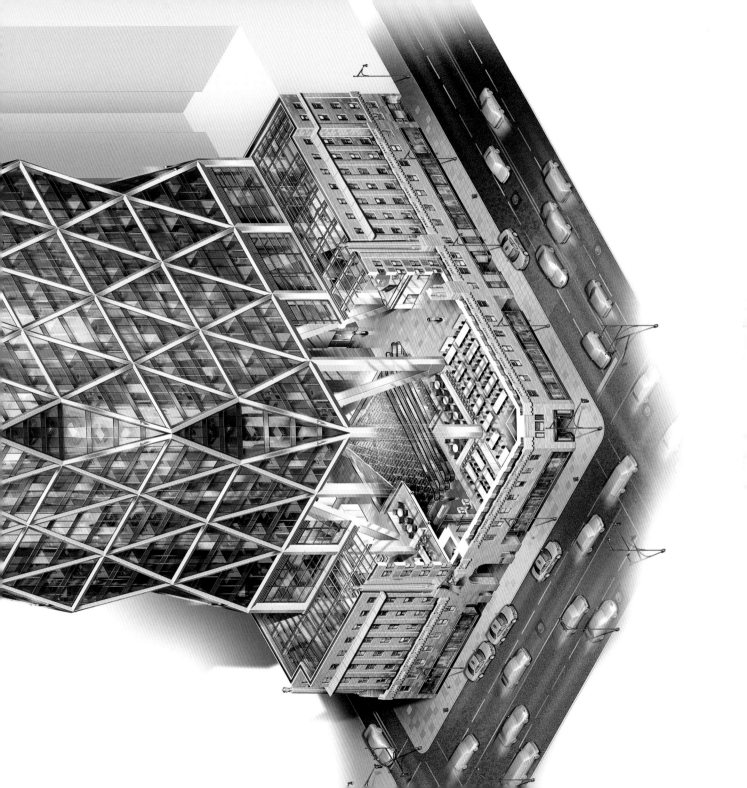

# Taking the city into the office Joseph Giovannini

New York, like nature, abhors a vacuum. For all the grandeur of its skyline, there are very few great public rooms in Manhattan. The city so defined by verticality remains, inside all those towers, spatially horizontal, organised in section like stacks of pancakes. That is because all the main forces that typically drive the building ecosystem – real estate maximisation, design assumptions, architectural typologies, construction convention, engineering practice and banking expectations – conspire to restrict if not eliminate their existence. There are, occasionally, buildings that vary the pancake stack enough to accommodate atria in their upper reaches, but such spaces are few and only rarely rooted in the building's fundamental concept. In this respect, as in many others, Hearst Tower is an exception.

Walk past the original building's meticulously restored facade between 56th and 57th Streets, and through the lobby at 959 Eighth Avenue, and a bank of escalators rises through sheets of cascading water to deliver you into a cavernous, six-storey volume beneath the new tower. It is a revelation of space, light and openness.

The original Hearst building, at the base of the tower, which occupies half a Manhattan block, masks the 3,600-square-metre lobby space on the third floor.

So for the first-time visitor its expansive presence at the top of the escalators comes as a complete surprise. V-shaped super columns at the corners and edges hold the tower 21 metres above the floor, which is otherwise free-span and column free. The elevator core serving this generous space lies off-centre, toward the western end of the building. For New Yorkers used to feeling spatially compressed inside towers as they pass from the lobby into elevators through corridors to their office modules, the space is an unexpected gift, and a major event in a city where majesty of space seems to be losing the battle against the bottom line.

The origins of this space can be traced back many years. The existing structure, grandly called the International Magazine Building, was commissioned by the media baron William Randolph Hearst who, by the late 1920s, had long put architecture to use to manifest his journalistic empire. Newspapers were local institutions, and Hearst appreciated how architecture could shape the perception of the newspapers in the communities they served, reinforcing their status and credibility. For a publisher whose enterprises thrived on declamatory headlines, architecture was rhetoric made permanent. In California, he commissioned Julia Morgan – who

Previous pages: Cutaway drawing. The tower rises above the shell of the original International Magazine Building, held aloft by V-shaped super columns. From the entrance on Eighth Avenue escalators rise to the sky-lit lobby which occupies the entire footprint of the old building.

Left: William Randolph Hearst (1863-1951) on the cover of *Time* magazine, 15 August 1927.

Right: Set designs for the Ziegfeld Follies by Joseph Urban (1872-1933). Urban trained as an architect, but is best known for his theatre work.

also designed his eclectic estate at San Simeon – to create the Herald Examiner Building in Los Angeles, where the tiled dome and reaching arms still bear impressive witness to the power of a newspaper that no longer exists. For Hearst, who saw the International Magazine Building as the company's spiritual home, the building was the flagship structure in his empire.

Hearst was always at the cutting edge of journalistic expansion, and with the emergence of national magazines early in the century, he wanted to build in Manhattan a structure that would not only house his growing stable of titles – he owned twelve magazines at the time – but also advertise their collective presence and the momentum of his journalistic power. A theatrical personality known to his colleagues as 'the chief' (memorably portrayed by Orson Wells in Citizen Kane), Hearst commissioned the expatriate Austrian architect and set designer Joseph Urban to design the new headquarters building in collaboration with George B Post & Sons. Urban, who was art director of Hearst's film-making studio, had remodelled the Criterion and Cosmopolitan theatres for Hearst, and designed the Ziegfeld Theater, which Hearst financed.

Post had significant experience designing office towers. Hearst cabled Urban that he wanted a building

of 'conspicuous architectural character'. The structure that resulted from their collaboration was a six-storey Art Deco building, U-shaped in plan, that was envisaged as the base of a nine-storey office tower to be built in a second phase. The base was an office block traditional in its massing and eclectic in its surface decoration. Allegorical figures representing music, commerce, art and industry sat atop pylons set around the centre and corner entrances. The base was organised so that the tower would be fitted in place at a later date, with building systems, such as vertical circulation, already aligned in the base structure, simply awaiting extension into the upper reaches.

From the early years of the twentieth century, Hearst had acquired several large parcels of land around 57th Street and Eighth Avenue, near Columbus Circle, anticipating that the area would become an extension of the city's burgeoning theatre district. He secured the site for the International Magazine Building in 1921. Its location meant that the new building would form a pivot between the theatre district and the site of the nearby Metropolitan Opera House, for which Joseph Urban was also preparing designs at the time. It would be another important element in a swathe of the city devoted to the arts and

Left: Commissioned by publishing magnate William Randolph Hearst and designed by Joseph Urban, the International Magazine Building was completed in 1928.

entertainment. Hearst's instincts proved prescient. The 'media mile' he predicted was finally consolidated with the construction of the Time Warner Center at Columbus Circle, and Hearst Tower is now the keystone he intended in that cultural arch through the city.

Designed during 1926-1927, the International Magazine Building was completed in 1928, but the Depression cut short ambitions for the tower. Still, the Hearst Corporation maintained the right to build a tower and Post returned to make proposals in 1945-1947 and file plans for a scheme, which was not built. (There are no drawings extant of the first tower, and no proof in fact that it was ever designed.)

Throughout the following decades, the Hearst Corporation continued to expand and diversify. By 2000, some 1,800 employees were scattered in nine office buildings in the area. The company owned some of the properties, and rented others. When the corporation decided to consolidate its New York operations under one roof, the idea of a tower above the Hearst building was resurrected. The new tower would be an expression of a newly invigorated phase in the corporation's development as it headed into the twenty-first century – architecture could do again what it had done for Hearst nearly a century before.

However, by that time the International Magazine Building was designated as an 'important monument in the architectural heritage of New York' and the preservation laws in the city, put in place after the demolition of Penn Station, were highly protective. The issue of adding to a historic monument was obviously sensitive, and required approval by the Landmarks Preservation Commission. According to New York preservation standards, a new structure in this context should express its own time yet respect and strengthen the original historic building, although any intervention should also be 'appropriate' to the original. Interestingly, the notion of 'appropriateness', a highly subjective issue, has stalled or defeated so many proposals in the fiercely contested space of Manhattan, where New Yorkers are famously territorial and resistant to change. Hearst was advised to search for an architect who could think outside conventional New York practice.

Hearst approached Foster + Partners because of the practice's considerable experience of making sympathetic interventions within historic structures. In the Reichstag in Berlin, for example, Foster renovated the historic shell and incorporated a soaring glass dome that has become a major landmark in the city. In London, the practice created the Great Court at

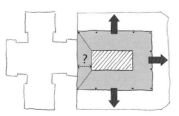

Left: Sketch exploring the relationship between Hearst Tower and The Sheffield apartment building (to the left).

Right: The design team explored many different massing options for the tower, which had to conform to a strictly enforced Manhattan zoning envelope.

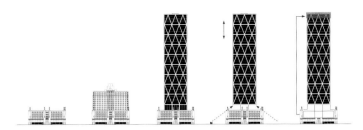

the British Museum, throwing a carapace of glass over an outdoor space to create an elegant atrium. But beyond the architects' successes at operating with almost surgical precision on historic buildings, the Foster team had cultivated specialties that would serve the Hearst project well.

Structure has emerged in Foster's practice not just as a metaphor for architectural order, but also as a salient feature of his systems-oriented designs. Rather than assuming conventional structural systems, Foster frequently reinvents them, and in association with other innovations, such as removing elevator cores from central positions in the plan, innovative structural engineering has in his hands proved spatially liberating. In the Hongkong and Shanghai Bank Headquarters, for example, Foster built a bridge-like structure, with trusses spanning between the corner towers. By doing so, he was able to open up the ground level as a sheltered plaza and create a soaring atrium and double-height floors within the building itself. The structure cracked open a section that would otherwise have been tightly closed, allowing space and light to flow freely through the building.

It is hard to overestimate the importance of the Hongkong Bank in the history of high-rise design. Foster's tutor at Yale, Paul Rudolph, was interested

in porous sections, and Rudolph himself was influenced by the spatial porosity of sections designed by Frank Lloyd Wright – for example, at the Larkin Building in Buffalo. But Rudolph basically sculpted interior space, and Wright used conventional structure. For Foster, structure has been the enabling instrument that opens form to volume.

In subsequent commissions, with different programmes in different climates and varying cultural circumstances, Foster pursued the idea of carving out significant interior spaces, and the porous sections became increasingly open, taking on an environmental role. The Commerzbank in Frankfurt, for example, has garden atria within a structure triangulated around a light-well that runs through the full height of the tower. The gardens provide the key to the building's natural ventilation system as well as forming social foci for groups of office floors – places to stop for a coffee or meet during breaks in the daily routine.

One of the defining characteristics of Foster's design method is the way the team develops a scheme through a systematic analysis of the problem. They do not approach a project with a priori solutions and geometries, but try to understand the commission in terms that will define its own design trajectory. The necessity of keeping, and featuring, the historic

structure played a major role in determining the Hearst Tower design, although it was but one factor in a far larger physical and commercial system of interrelated concerns.

The historical outer wall, which the architects were required to preserve, was the first of several issues to be resolved. Compositionally, it was determined that the old Hearst building would act as a 'plinth' to the tower on top – as originally envisaged by Urban and Post. However, the existing U-shaped building was configured around an off-set courtyard whose fourth side was formed by the service core of an adjacent residential tower, The Sheffield. Thus the six-storey plinth threatened to overwhelm the lower storeys of a tower planted in the hollow of the 'U', severely restricting daylight penetration. On the other hand, had the lower floors been reconfigured to fill in the courtyard, the resulting floor plates would have had an impracticable depth ratio from window to core.

There was a further complication. The usual assumption of a free-standing tower is that it is four-sided, with perimeters open to the view on all sides in a pattern of rising desirability: the higher the floor, the longer the view, the greater the prestige. However, The Sheffield was built to the common north-south property line, and therefore would have

**The Hearst Tower scored decisive points because it is more than a refinement of an existing type. It is really a prototype.** Michaela Busenkell, curator at the Deutsches Architekturmuseum, describing the conclusions of the jury for the 2008 International Highrise Award, *Architectural Record*, November 2008

Above left: An early 1:200-scale presentation model of the final scheme.

Right: Model makers in the Foster studio at work on study models of the tower's facade and structure.

Left: Diagrams illustrating
alternative structural treatments:
diagrid versus post and beam.
The efficiency of the diagrid
system means that it uses
20 per cent less steel than
a conventional frame.

blocked the view of any west-facing facade for most of the height of the building. The solution was to let The Sheffield lift core exert a magnetic pull on the Hearst core. The architects moved the core to the extreme west of the site, in effect laminating it to The Sheffield. This displacement had a liberating effect on the eastern part of the tower. The office floors, which no longer had to circle the core, could be completely open from window wall to window wall, giving considerable planning flexibility.

There were further forces acting on the placement of the tower. Because the floor heights of the Art Deco building were unsuited to contemporary office space, and because the lower floors of the tower would lose light if nested within the existing courtyard, the height of the 'plinth' building tended to push the base of the tower up to a height where it would not only clear the top of the plinth, but also float above it. Articulating the plinth and the tower from each other had the potential for creating a very tall, light-filled space within the plinth that could be ringed by clerestory windows. Separating the old building from the new tower with a horizontal spatial reveal also solved the issue of how to design the transition from the 'heavy' masonry base to the 'light' glass-and-steel superstructure. The two structures represented a change of era, a different

attitude to materials and structure. It was therefore a difficult but important transition to resolve.

The decision to align the core with that of The Sheffield, presented an engineering challenge, because the decentred core could not stabilise the entire tower as it would in a conventional structure. To compensate for the displaced core, the architects needed to devise a structural system that could provide compensatory bracing on the eastern side of the tower.

Foster + Partners actively pursues research and development programmes through its commissions. This manifests itself in different ways. For example, the diagrid (a conflation of 'diagonal' and 'grid') structure developed for Hearst emerged as a very practical solution because it provides greater strength and greater structural redundancy, using 20 per cent less steel than a conventional post-and-beam structure – a saving of approximately 2,000 tonnes of steel. It could also be deployed as an exoskeleton, thus keeping the interiors relatively free of columns. Additionally, the frame was constructed using 85 per cent recycled steel, which has a considerable impact in terms of the building's embodied energy.

Foster has never taken established building typologies as fixes; instead he likes to look at a

Right: In this early model, built to study the base of the tower and the arrangement of the lobby, the escalators rise from entrance level through an oval cut in the lobby floor.

problem from first principles, allowing the physical givens of a particular programme or site to suggest a process of inquiry. As Foster says: 'Over time, we've accumulated a body of knowledge and a continued thirst to explore what makes a building – and that has a very strong research component. That curiosity extends to every aspect of the building – how it's constructed, how it's assembled, the materials used, the potential those materials might have to adapt to new uses, and so on. It's really a series of parallel explorations in terms of what generates the need for the building and how that building is in turn realised.'

The unique characteristics of the site in this case acted as determinants in a process that was, by its physical logic, self-organising if not self-designing. Interestingly, Foster's scheme sailed through the approvals process, aided by the fact that Urban's structure was always intended as the base for a tower (and the fact that there was no record of any of his design intentions).

The architects were encouraged in their open-minded search by the desire of the Hearst Corporation to stake out creative ground in the New York skyline with a tower whose profile characterised the company itself as progressive and forward thinking, ready to take on a new century. Hearst enjoys great corporate

independence because it is privately held rather than publicly traded and can therefore venture beyond conventional real-estate wisdom without having to account to shareholders. As a private corporation, Hearst was looking to the future from the position of an established and successful past and the new building would reflect that.

The tower that New Yorkers see today is a unique diamond-gridded web whose stainless-steel members form a thirty-four-storey structural tube arranged in a diagrid eight tiers high: each tier is composed of sequentially paired triangles four storeys high. Where the grid turns the corners at a 45 degree angle, the structure opens up to form what the architects call a 'bird's mouth' (each corner has four birds' mouths), which together have the effect of creating a change of rhythm at each corner of the tower. The glazing on the upper half of each bird's mouth leans forwards and that on the lower half inwards. Consequently, floor plates vary, both in the distance across the breadth of the 'mouth', and in the inclination of the glass. Inside, the architects dedicate each corner to a public use, and the corners allow unobstructed, panoramic views that are diagonal to the city, a view that is all the more dramatic in the upper part of the cut, which positions viewers as though they were in the gondola of an

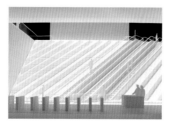

Left: A sketch model of 'Icefall' made by the design team to explore the diagonal configuration of the escalators.

**Hearst Tower is both a product for a corporate client and a broader experiment attempting to confront global ecological problems through design. The tension between these identities helps generate its interest and its influence.** Bill Millard, *Icon*, May 2006

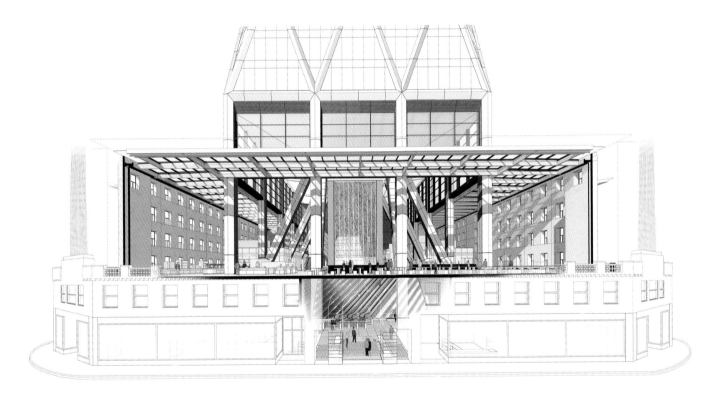

Above: Perspective section showing the entrance sequence from Eighth Avenue; the International Magazine Building's original vaulted entrance hall has been maintained. From there visitors and staff ascend to lobby level via banks of escalators.

airship, or the bubble of a helicopter, looking down. Individual floors range from 1,580 square metres to 1,860 square metres, and each is occupied by a magazine or a corporate department. On the top floor – reserved for meetings and receptions – there is a triple-height space in each corner plus one in the centre, which opens eastwards to offer a sweeping panorama of the city.

The architects evolved the structural design in association with structural engineer Ahmad Rahimian, of the US engineering firm Cantor Seinuk. The tower as a shaft is structurally unique within New York, and while it is by no means the first exoskeletal steel structure, it represents – after Swiss Re – one of the first applications of the diagrid at large scale. (Foster subsequently proposed a similar system for his twin towers in the competition to rebuild the World Trade Center.)

The uniqueness of the diagrid translates in New York into an iconic image for Hearst, within a skyline that is highly competitive. What distinguishes the Hearst Tower is that the iconic quality is not achieved through the crown but the shaft, along its entire length, and even then the shaft is not figural but systematically triangulated and regular. The triangulation, which creates a self-bracing structure, eliminates the need

Above left: Perspective studies of a double-height executive area (top) and a corner editorial office on the upper levels of the tower, with the view across New York as a backdrop.

Right: Study models of a typical office floor showing proposed office layouts. The offset core generates a U-shaped floor plate, with a large open area to the east. Glass-walled cellular offices are arranged around the perimeter of each floor, with support areas inboard.

for the diagonal bracing that can often be seen threaded through conventional structural frames. Additionally, the efficiency of the exoskeleton eliminates almost entirely the need for internal columns (there are only two on each floor, required because the displaced elevator core lengthened the open floor plates significantly in the east-west direction).

Another significant strand in the development of the building is that it was one of the first in the United States to integrate energy efficient design and concerns about sustainability in a large-scale environment. Like other progressive companies, Hearst understands the concept of a healthy workplace – something that will become increasingly important in terms of staff recruitment in the future. Indeed, Hearst's experience with the green building process may herald the more widespread construction of environmentally sensitive buildings in the city.

Hearst's building has been designed to use 25 per cent less energy than it would had it minimally complied with the respective state and city energy codes. This has earned it a gold certification under the US Green Building Council's Leadership in Energy and Environmental Design (LEED). It was the first occupied building in New York to receive this certification and it reinforces Foster's observation that it is owner-occupiers – of the likes of Willis Faber, the Hongkong Bank and the Commerzbank – who can be relied upon to pioneer innovation, often setting new standards that will later be adopted by the market.

This effort required not only intelligent structural and environmental engineering but the introduction of high-performance materials and integrated systems that can achieve a very high degree of operational efficiency. For example, the tower's glazing incorporates a low-emissivity glass that allows the offices to be flooded with light while blocking solar radiation; sensors on each floor control artificial lighting levels, and switch off lights when a room is vacant; and the building's heating and air-conditioning equipment utilises outside air for cooling and ventilation for approximately 75 per cent of the year, a move that not only saves energy but improves air quality. The reduction in electrical energy use that these systems bring is estimated at 2 million kWh, which will save 900 tonnes of carbon dioxide annually – the equivalent, the engineers say, of taking 180 cars off New York's streets.

Efforts are also made to conserve water. The roof harvests rainfall, which is stored in basement reclamation tanks. This 'grey' water replaces water lost to evaporation in the air-conditioning systems

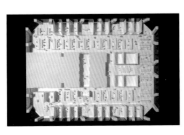 

and irrigates planting and trees inside and outside the building, and supplies the water feature in the lobby.

The lay audience may not understand and appreciate the building's environmental science or engineering per se, but the tower's daring structure piques curiosity and an involvement with its architecture through questioning. Looking up, you have to ask yourself: 'if corners stabilise a structure, how does a building without corners stand?'

At ground level, the perception is more settled. Foster affirms the traditional New York urbanism by restoring the existing perimeter wall and maintaining its intimate relationship with the street. The old arched entrance and lobby to the Hearst building remains where it always was, on Eighth Avenue, and shops occupy the rest of the street frontage. The architects kept only the facade of the old structure, one bay in and two storeys tall, for retail, with the remainder of the floor plate dedicated to back-of-house services. The third through to the sixth floors have been removed, and the perimeter wall, stuccoed on the inside, now defines a new space starting on the third floor, which forms the building's lobby. The steel frame that originally supported the six-storey building has been entirely removed, except for a bay that stabilises the limestone facade. By cutting a new subway entrance

through the building and otherwise improving the subway station itself, Hearst earned the right to add an additional six floors to the tower.

The Hearst lobby is an interior urbanism of a daring scale. A building with 79,500 square metres in forty-four storeys houses roughly 2,000 people – the equivalent of a small town – all of whom have business in common. New York skyscrapers are notorious for isolating workers within elevator cars, in corridors and in cubicles. With Hearst, in contrast, by separating the tower from the base, Foster creates a huge volume of 'found' space that he dedicates for public use in order to socialise the building. It is the equivalent of a campus quad, or watering hole, or as Foster says, 'a town square', an urban room designed to encourage a sense of identity and community.

In designing this space, the architects have taken great care to create an environment where people meet casually, linger, chat, and perhaps transact a little business. The lobby contains the Joseph Urban auditorium and the building's primary restaurant, Cafe 57, so that it acts as a powerful social magnet. The space is also configured so that it forms an essential part of the route into the building, through which people disembarking from the escalators walk to the elevators that will take them to the upper floors.

Below left: Looking up at
the tower as the frame nears
completion; the cladding
and glazing are progressing
in sequence.

Below right: Construction
workers install one of
the Y-nodes, which form
the connecting pieces
in the diagrid structure.

Far left: Within the facade of
the old International Magazine
Building the structure was
demolished and excavated
down to bedrock; the facade is
shown here with its temporary
supporting structure.

Left: Looking down into the
lobby from the lower deck of
the tower. The steel V-shaped
super columns that support the
tower are filled with concrete
reinforcement.

Construction was rapid: ground
was broken in April 2003; the
steel frame was topped out on
11 February 2005; the building
was finished by March 2006;
and staff moved in during May.
On completion it was recognised
as the first 'green' commercial
building in Manhattan, awarded
a Gold LEED rating from the
US Green Building Council.

**At forty-four storeys, the Hearst is modest by New York standards; yet even in a city crowded with skyscrapers it stands out. The diamond panels slant in and out, touching at just five points, every eight floors. It works the magic trick of abolishing corners.** Deyan Sudjic, *The Observer*, 8 January 2006

Below: The artist Richard Long was commissioned to create a site-specific art work for the lobby. The result – RIVERLINES – is made from mud 'harvested' from the Avon and Hudson rivers and is described by the artist as a 'cave painting for the twenty-first century'.

Right: Richard Long at work on RIVERLINES; although it was many months in the planning, the piece was completed in just three days, from 26 to 28 April 2006.

Far right: Norman Foster, on a site visit to the Hearst lobby, waves to Richard Long.

Overleaf: Hearst Tower glimpsed from the Hudson River; though it is far from being the tallest building in Manhattan its profile is very distinctive.

Sitting in the cafeteria, employees look up through the perimeter skylights and see the exterior of the tower on one side and the wall of the original building by Urban on the other. At night, the clerestory windows are lit, creating a band of light on which the tower seems magically to rest. Illuminated from within at night, the tower, with its basket weave, looks like a lantern.

The lobby is also the scene of two significant collaborations with artists. The first of these, with the glass specialist Jamie Carpenter and Jim Garland of Fluidity, has resulted in the creation of 'Icefall'. The escalators rise diagonally between a three-storey cascade of water, which plays over a series of cast-glass prisms that capture and refract light. 'The water sparkles with sunlight, just as it would in nature', says Foster. 'Icefall' also has an environmental function, circulating harvested water to humidify the atrium in winter and cool it in summer.

Reaching the top of the escalator visitors are confronted with a second work – Richard Long's RIVERLINES – a tall mural set against the grey stone of the lift core. Like 'a cave painting for the twenty-first century', it is made from mud 'harvested' from the banks of the Avon and Hudson rivers and celebrates the metaphor of the river as a symbol of journey, movement and life.

Impressive as these two pieces are, by far the most striking feature of the space is the volume itself. It is the latest in a long line of social spaces that Foster has conceived in tall office buildings, from the Hongkong Bank and the Commerzbank to Swiss Re. In each case he rejects the notion of collecting workers at the same address only to disperse them within the isolating layers of the usual pancake office floors. Surely, he argues, that defeats the potential of creating a community of co-workers, and developing the networking and synergies possible across a large corporation.

With Hearst, Foster has designed a plan and section that gather people under the same roof in the same space: this is an arena of collaboration, and perhaps the best argument against balkanising workers in home offices linked by the computer. Hearst's corporate agora is designed to make the experience of the city and the office simultaneously more liveable, enjoyable and productive.

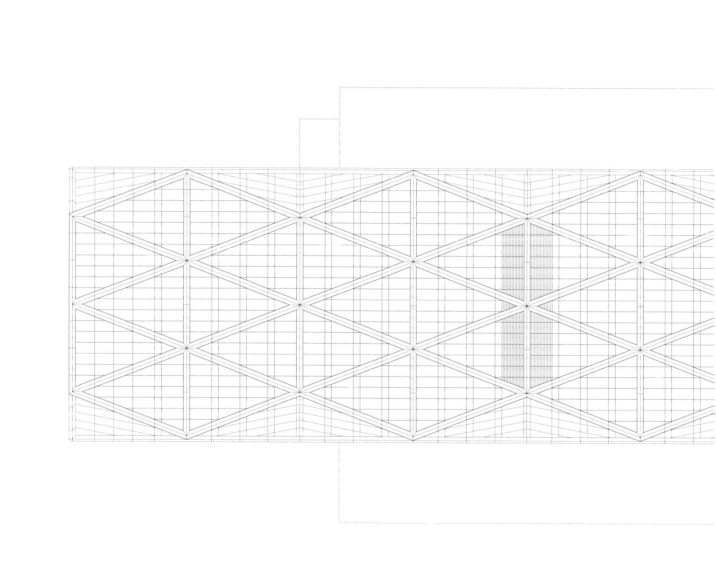

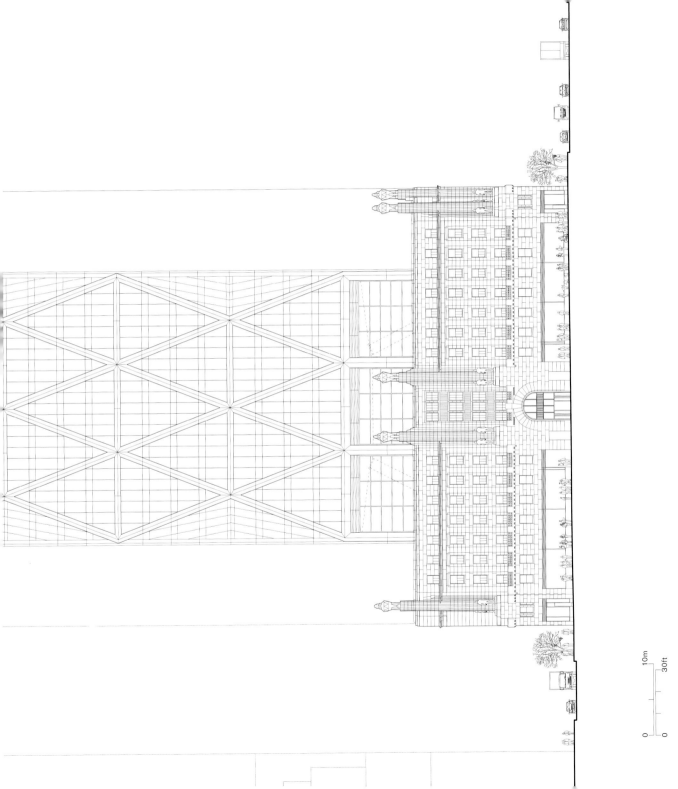

10m

30ft

0

0

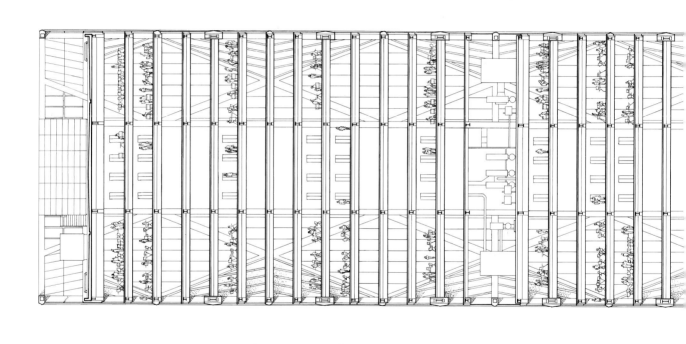

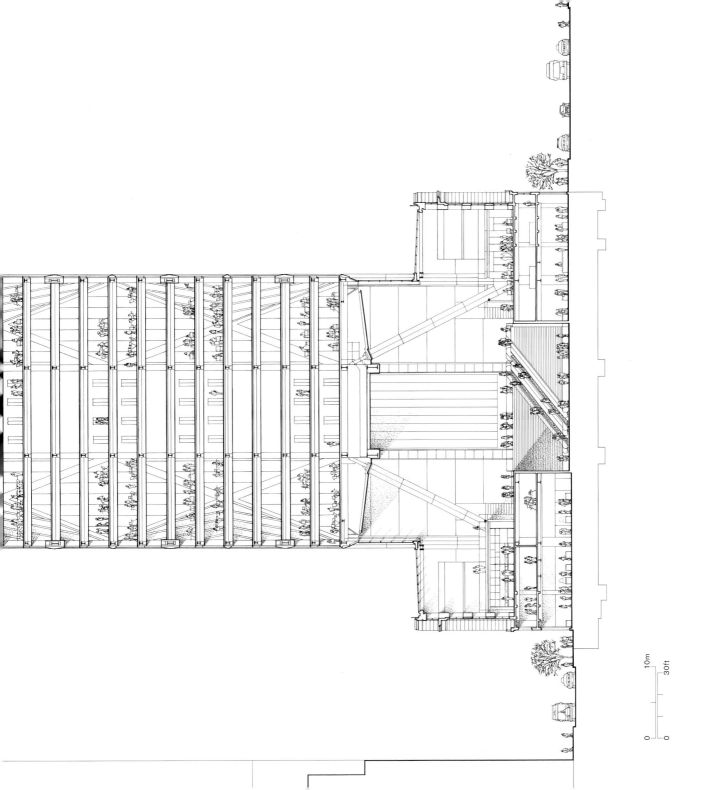

10m

30ft

0

0

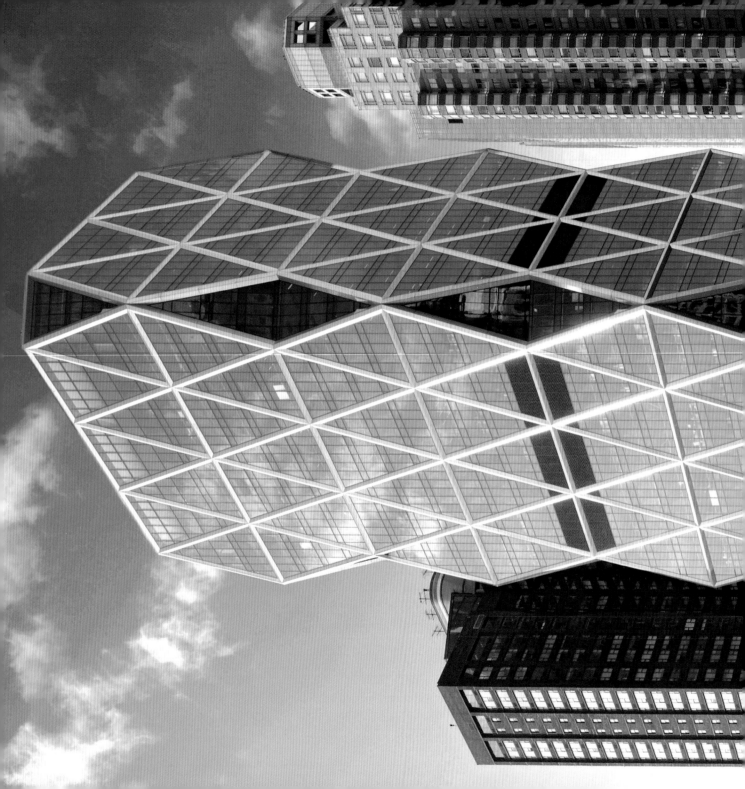

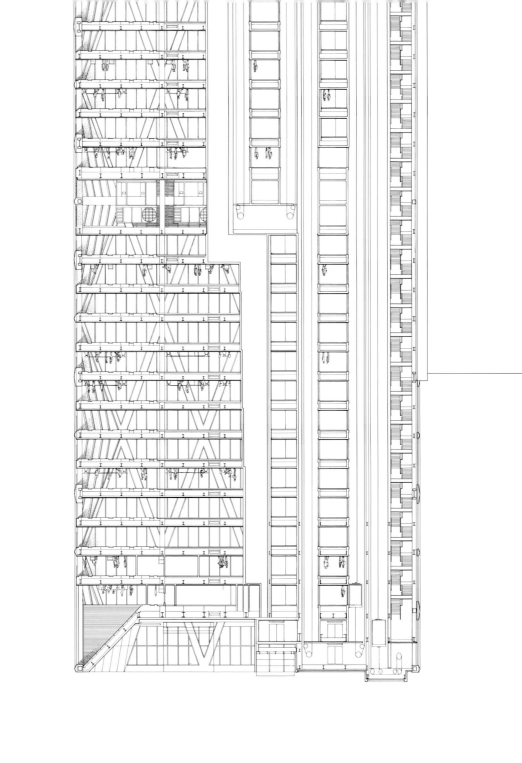

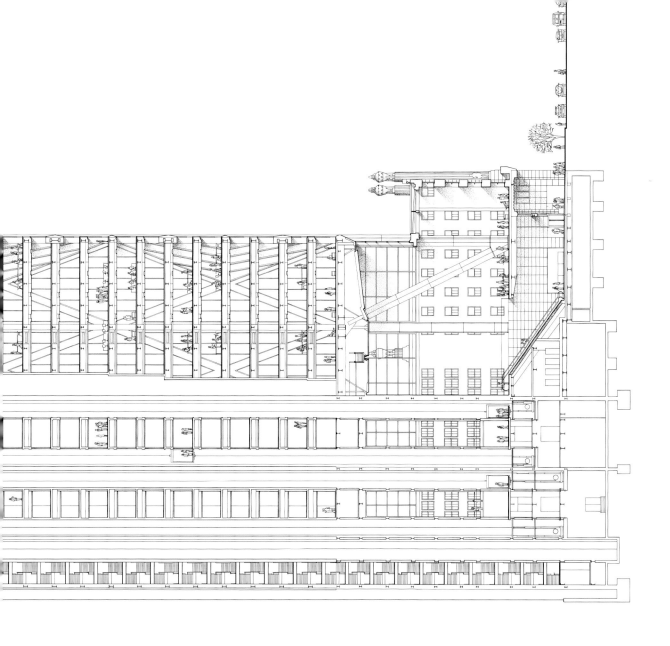

10m
30ft
0
0

Above: Hearst Tower approached from Eighth Avenue.

Right: A detail of the facade; each triangle in the diagrid is four storeys high. High-performance, low-emission glazing allows internal spaces to be naturally lit while blocking solar radiation, which would cause heat gain.

**This is not just a convincing piece of sculpture and structural logic: it is equally a piece of contextualism, and of historic preservation, that makes a strong contribution to the vitality of the city.** Deyan Sudjic, *The Observer*, 8 January 2006

Hearst Tower seen from the
Sheep Meadow in Central Park.

Left: Because of its central
Manhattan location, the tower is
seen fleetingly or obliquely rather
than viewed in the round.

Above: Old and new juxtaposed.
From this viewpoint, the tower's
faceted corners greatly enhance
its vertical emphasis.

Above: Hearst Tower seen from Columbus Circle.

Right: A building without corners in the conventional sense, its facades meet in a series of eight-storey-high 'birds' mouths'.

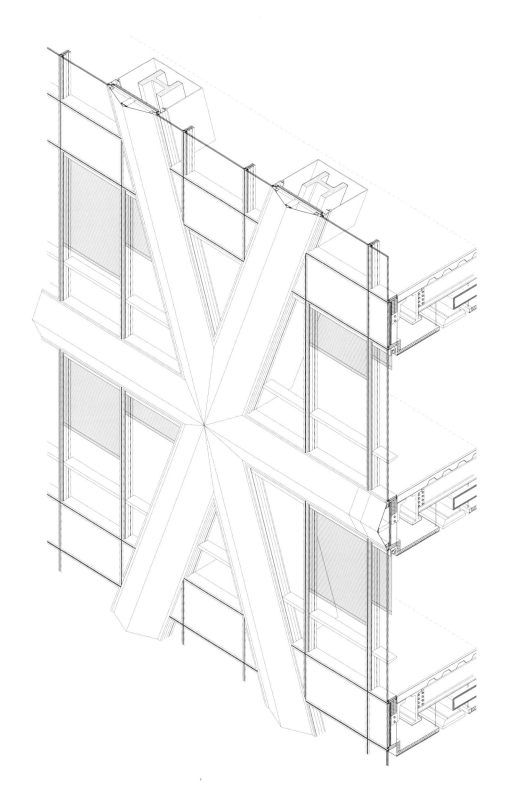

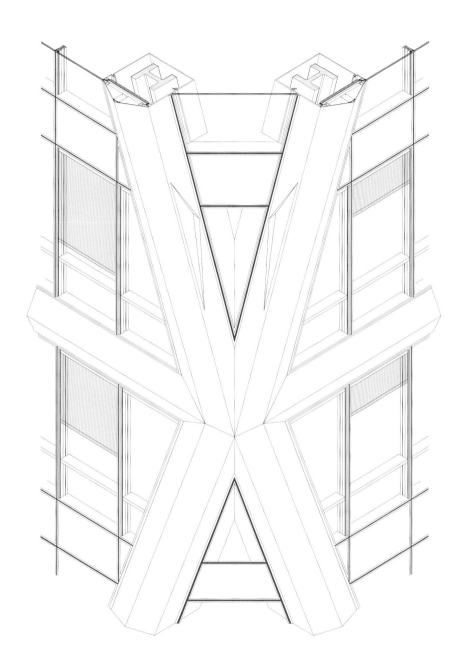

Opposite: An isometric projection of a typical intersection in the tower's structural diagrid. The diagrid comprises a series of four-storey high frames, each 6.6 metres (54 feet) tall.

Left: The corresponding corner detail. The external cladding is profiled stainless steel.

A detail of the facade, with its triangulated frame. Hearst Tower is unique in Manhattan in having no vertical framing members.

As with all Foster designs, the Hearst Tower is sleek, refined and filled with new technology. It looks nothing like the Jazz Age confection on which it sits. The addition is sheathed in glass and stainless steel – a shiny missile shooting out of Joseph Urban's stone launching pad. Paul Goldberger, *The New Yorker*, 19 December 2005

Above and right: The original
facade by Joseph Urban is of
cast stone. The upper four floors
are set back from the base with
massive piers that accentuate
the building's height. The
sculptural scheme by Henry Kreis
features six groups of allegorical
figures representing music, art,
commerce and industry.

Left: At night, the building's internal logic is revealed.

Above: The building is entered through the original entrance arch at 959 Eighth Avenue. Historically, the street level was given over to shops and showrooms – a tradition that has been maintained.

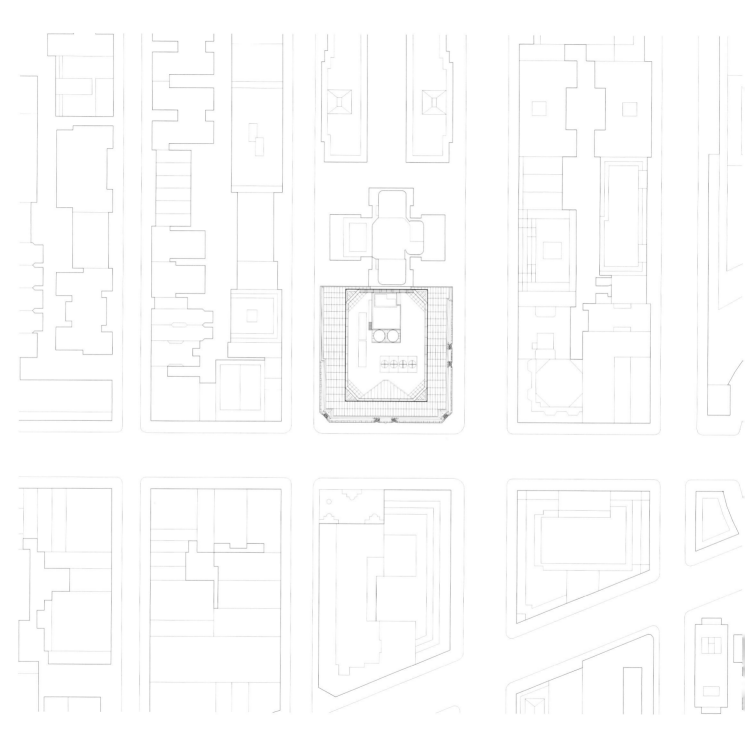

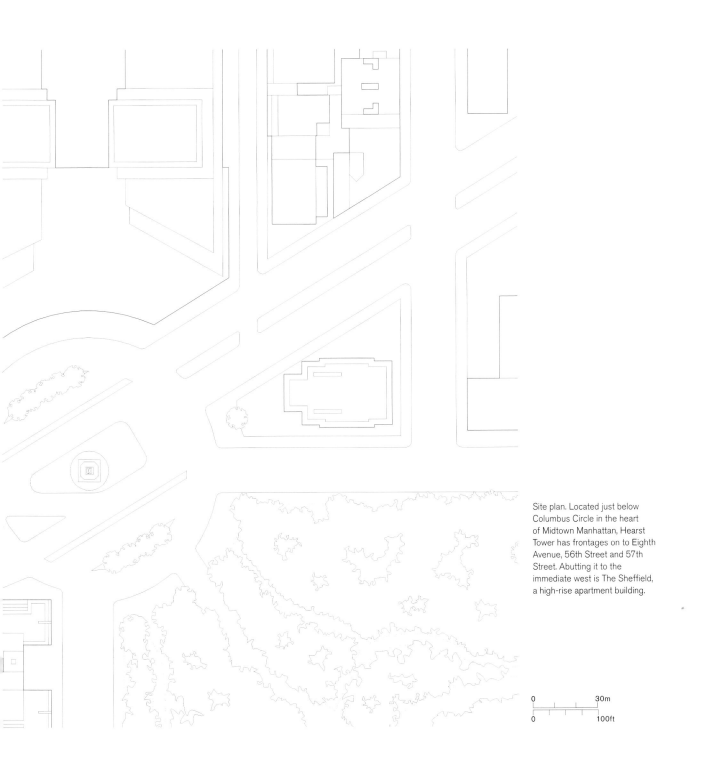

Site plan. Located just below Columbus Circle in the heart of Midtown Manhattan, Hearst Tower has frontages on to Eighth Avenue, 56th Street and 57th Street. Abutting it to the immediate west is The Sheffield, a high-rise apartment building.

0          30m

0          100ft

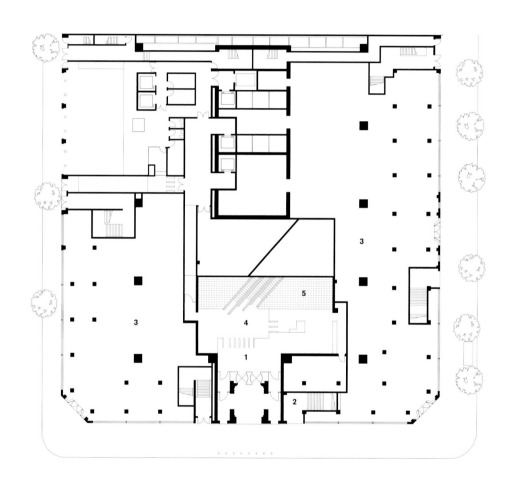

0          10m
0          30ft

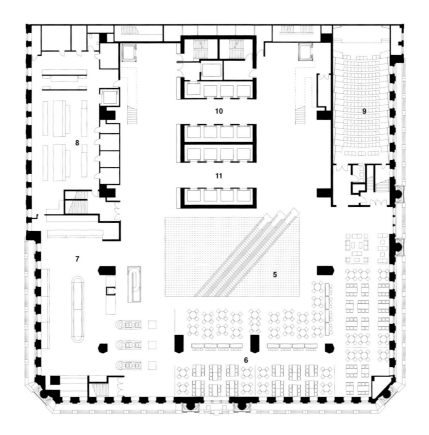

Left: Plan at entrance level

Above: Plan at lobby level

1 reception
2 subway entrance
3 retail space
4 lobby
5 'Icefall'
6 Café 57
7 servery

8 kitchen
9 Joseph Urban auditorium
10 high-rise elevators
11 low-rise elevators

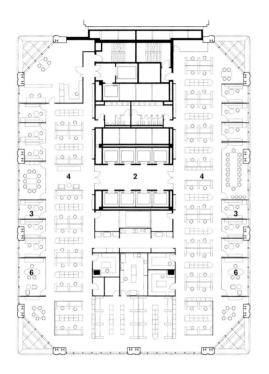

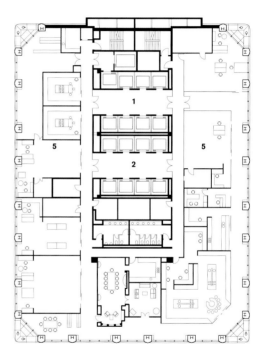

Left: A typical lower-level office floor.

Right: The Good Housekeeping Research Institute on Level 28.

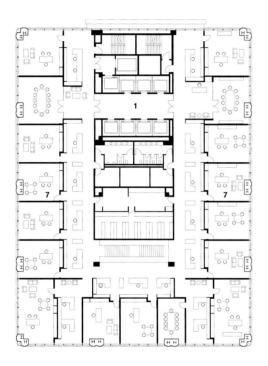

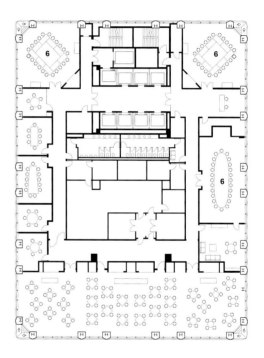

Left: The executive floor
on Level 40

Right: Boardrooms and executive
break-out spaces on Level 41

1 high-rise elevators
2 low-rise elevators
3 cellular offices
4 open-plan offices
5 Good Housekeeping
  Research Institute
6 meeting room
7 executive offices

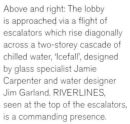

Above and right: The lobby is approached via a flight of escalators which rise diagonally across a two-storey cascade of chilled water, 'Icefall', designed by glass specialist Jamie Carpenter and water designer Jim Garland. RIVERLINES, seen at the top of the escalators, is a commanding presence.

You go in through Urban's original
arch — which has been meticulously
restored — and up a set of escalators.
What comes next is an explosive
surprise such has not been seen in
the city since Frank Lloyd Wright led
people through a low, tight lobby
into the rotunda of the Guggenheim.

Paul Goldberger, *The New Yorker*,
19 December 2005

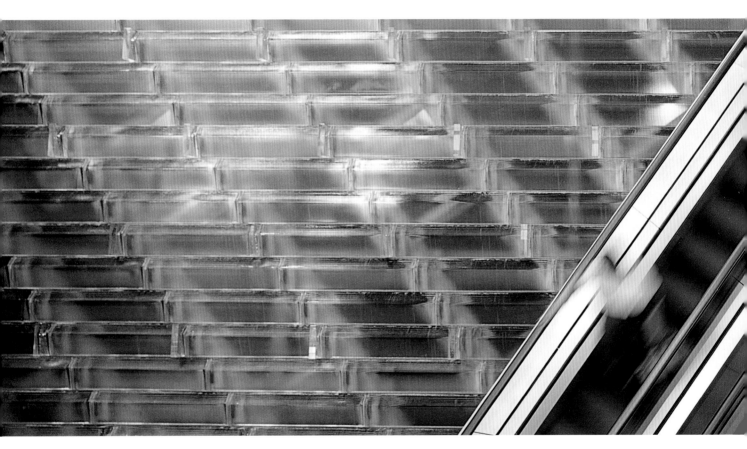

A detail of the escalators and 'Icefall'. The waterfall plays an environmental role, reusing collected rainwater to cool the atrium in summer and humidify the space in winter.

**Hearst Tower is a statement about who we are as a company, the confidence with which we view the future in a changing world of media, and about our place in this great city.**
Victor F Ganzi, former Hearst Corporation President and CEO, speaking at the opening ceremony, 8 October 2006

Above: The walls of the lobby reflect the cast stone of the facade in tone and colour, creating a conscious ambiguity between inside and outside.

Right: The tower is raised six storeys above the floor of the lobby on V-shaped super columns.

Left: The view up through the glass 'skirt' that spans between the old building and the tower and forms the roof of the lobby.

Below: Looking down towards the street entrance from the mezzanine level gallery.

Overleaf: Standing in the lobby, looking south; there is the impression of being in a bustling town square rather than a conventional office lobby.

**I visited the building just as the first 'Hearsties' were moving in. A storm front came in just as we reached the top, and I felt like Zeus. Water poured on to the roof shelves of the atrium. It seemed as though we were on a ship in a storm – it was thrilling.**
Joseph Giovannini, in conversation with the editor, 2006

Left: Hearst employees enjoying a break in the staff restaurant, Café 57.

Above: Looking across the lobby to the self-service food-counter.

Above and right: Each floor
within the tower typically houses
a single magazine or publication.
Editorial meeting rooms are
placed around the perimeter
and in the 'birds' mouths' at
the corners.

**Norman has a feel for what it is
your business does. The dialogue
is often not about architecture, but
how does your business function,
and how do people live in the space.**
Frank A Bennack Jr, Hearst Corporation
Vice Chairman and CEO, *New York Times*,
19 June 2006

Above and right: The Good Housekeeping Research Institute has a range of specialist facilities, including state-of-the-art kitchens and food preparation spaces together with archive and product display areas, located on Level 28 immediately below the mid-level plant area.

The Good Housekeeping Research Institute's annual Good Buy Awards salute ingenious new products that help you every day.

Above and right: The editorial offices of *House Beautiful* and *Seventeen* magazines. Hearst is one of the world's largest magazine publishers, with fifteen US titles and nearly 200 international editions.

special
interest
publications

Left: Looking into the offices
of *Harper's Bazaar* – America's
oldest fashion magazine, whose
distinguished contributors have
included Diana Vreeland and
Alexey Brodovitch.

Above: An editorial conference
taking place in one of the
glass-walled offices.

Below: An executive office on Level 42; each executive was encouraged to choose his or her own furnishings.

Right: A double-height executive break-out space on Level 42.

**Joseph Urban's goal in the original Hearst building was to create a respectable form of flamboyance, and Foster has figured out how to do the same thing with his tower, but in unquestionably modern terms, and without compromising his commitment to structural innovation.**
Paul Goldberger, *The New Yorker*, 19 December 2005

Overleaf: Hearst Tower at night
– a landmark in Manhattan.

# Facts and figures

**Hearst Tower**
New York, USA
2000–2006
Client
Hearst Corporation
Project Team (Building)
Norman Foster
Brandon Haw
David Nelson
Mike Jelliffe
Michael Wurzel
Peter Han

Bob Atwal
John Ball
Nick Baker
Una Barac
Gerard Evenden
Morgan Fleming
Michaela Koster
Chris Lepine
Martina Meluzzi
Julius Streifeneder
Gonzalo Surroca

Project Team (Fit-out)
Norman Foster
Brandon Haw
Mike Jelliffe
Chris West

Sandor Ambrus
Mandy Edge
Peter Han
Nasrin Kalbasi
John Small
Ingrid Solken
Kathleen Streifender
Michael Wurzel

Consultants
Associate Architects: Shell and core:
Adamson Associates; Fit-out:
Gensler
Development Manager: Tishman
Speyer Properties
Structural Engineer: Cantor Seinuk
Group
Services/MEP: Flack & Kurtz
Vertical Transportation: VDA
Lighting: George Sexton (shell and
core); Kugler Associates (fit-out)
Food Service: Ira Beer Associates
Main Contractor: Turner Construction

Principal Awards
2004 Wallpaper Design Awards
Winner Best Building Sites
2005 Global Green USA Green
Building Design Award
2006 Build New York Awards,
Winner New Project
2006 Emporis 'Best New
Skyscraper of the Year for
Design and Functionality'
2007 BCI International Award
2007 Business Week/Architectural
Record Citation for Excellence
for the Interiors
2007 RIBA International Award
2007 Archi Tech AV Awards,
Best Project over $1,000,000
2007 The Greater New York
Construction User Council
Outstanding Green Project Award
2007 New York City MASterwork
Awards, Best New Building
2007 AIA New York Design Honor
Award in the Architecture category

## Project chronology

1988  The Hearst Corporation's International Magazine Building is designated a Landmark Site by the New York City Landmarks Preservation Commission

2000  November: the Hearst Corporation commissions Foster + Partners to design a tower to rise above the existing Art Deco building

2001  Scheme design

2002  Detail design

2003  March: construction documents are issued; demolition begins 30 April: a groundbreaking ceremony is held; Hearst Tower is the first tall building to break ground in New York after 9/11

2005  11 February: to mark the placement of the highest steel beam, 597 feet (184 metres) above ground, the building is 'topped out'

2006  March: construction is completed 26 to 28 April: Richard Long completes RIVERLINES in the lobby May: the first Hearst employees move into the building 8 October: the building is officially opened

## Vital statistics

Location
  959 Eighth Avenue, New York, NY 10019

Gross area
  856,000 square feet/79,500 square metres

Net usable area
  650,218 square feet/60,470 square metres

Zoning area
  721,000 square feet/67,000 square metres (120,000 square feet/11,000 square metres from subway bonus)

Typical gross floor area
  20,000 square feet/1,900 square metres

Lobby gross floor area
  38,750 square feet/3,600 square metres

Roof area
  17,000 square feet/1,663 square metres

Typical floor-to-floor height
  13.5 feet/4.15 metres

Building height
  597 feet/182 metres

Total number of storeys
  44

Number of floors in the tower
  34

Building capacity
  1,800 – 2,200 people (the building brings together 2,000 New York based employees from ten locations)

Lifts/elevators
  15 passenger lifts incorporating destination based technology (seven high-rise, eight low-rise); two passenger lifts serve the mezzanine floors; there are two freight/service lifts

Structural system
  Steel core with perimeter diagonal structural system (diagrid) forming four-storey triangular frames. Concrete-reinforced steel super-columns up to tenth floor. No horizontal steel beams were used – a first for a North American office tower. Each triangle in the diagrid is 54 feet/16.6 metres tall

Structural steel tonnage
  10,480 tonnes

Cladding
  External cladding of diagrid is stainless steel; glazing is high-performance low emission glass

Cooling system
  Central air HVAC system at Level 28 with basement and roof-top mechanical equipment rooms

In addition to offices, the building contains a full-service television studio, state-of-the-art laboratory and test kitchens, a fitness centre, auditorium and a café/restaurant

The lobby varies in height between 40 and 70 feet (12.3 and 21.5 metres) and contains the staff cafeteria, an exhibition space and auditorium. It is accessed from Eighth Avenue through the existing vaulted entrance hall via escalators set within the three-storey water feature 'Icefall'

'Icefall' was designed in collaboration with the glass specialist Jamie Carpenter and Jim Garland of Fluidity

RIVERLINES, a 40x70 feet mural in the lobby, was created by the artist Richard Long using mud collected from the Avon and Hudson rivers

## Energy and ecology

Hearst Tower was the first 'green' occupied commercial building in New York City: it received a Gold Rating under the Leadership in Energy and Environmental Design (LEED) by the US Green Building Council

The building is designed to use 25 per cent less energy than an equivalent office building that complies minimally with the respective state and city codes

Over 85 per cent of the structural steel is recycled material

The diagrid frame of the tower uses approximately 20 per cent less steel than would a conventional perimeter frame – saving approximately 2,000 tonnes of steel

High-performance, low-emission glazing allows internal spaces to be naturally lit while blocking solar radiation, which would cause heat gain

Light sensors control the amount of artificial light on each floor based on the amount of natural light available at any given time; motion sensors allow lights and computers to be turned off when a room is vacant

High-efficiency heating and air-conditioning equipment utilises outside air for cooling and ventilation for 75 per cent of the year

The roof is designed to collect rainwater, which is stored in a 14,000-gallon reclamation tank located in the basement. Rainwater is used to replace water lost to evaporation in the office air-conditioning system; it is also used to irrigate plants inside and outside the building. Harvested water is also utilised for 'Icefall', the water feature in the grand atrium, whose environmental function is to humidify and chill the atrium lobby as required

Electrically actuated taps/faucets reduce water use by 25 per cent

Foreign-sourced materials account for less than 10 per cent of the total construction cost

## Building history

The six-storey Art-Deco International Magazine Building, located at 959 Eighth Avenue, between 56th and 57th Streets, was commissioned by the publishing magnate William Randolph Hearst (1863-1951)

Hearst envisaged a headquarters building as early as 1895 and began purchasing property in the Columbus Circle area. He secured at least six midtown properties as potential sites for the headquarters and finally purchased the present building's site in 1921

Hearst expected Columbus Circle to become the extension of New York's growing theatre district. Carnegie Hall at 57th Street and Seventh Avenue had been built in 1891 and in 1923 the Metropolitan Opera announced plans to construct a new opera house on 57th Street. The Opera's plans were abandoned but Columbus Circle experienced unprecedented commercial growth in the 1920s nonetheless

The International Magazine Building was designed by Joseph Urban with George B Post & Sons to convey the fact that 'it houses industries whose purpose is to exert influence on the thought and education of the reading public.' It was also designed to complement other music and arts buildings originally planned for the area

Construction began in 1927 and was completed in 1928 at a cost of $2 million

From the beginning, the six-storey building was structurally reinforced to become the base of a later office tower. Between 1945-1947 George B Post & Sons made proposals for nine additional storeys to be built above the original building; plans were filed in 1946 but never executed

Joseph Urban (1872-1933) was an Austrian émigré who trained as an architect but is best known for his theatre work. Urban became art director of Hearst's new film making studio, remodelled the Criterion and Cosmopolitan theatres for him and designed the Hearst-financed Ziegfeld Theater while serving as a set designer for the Metropolitan Opera. Most of Urban's architectural work has been demolished, the base of the Hearst building being a rare exception

George B Post & Sons was the architect of William Randolph Hearst's rival Joseph Pulitzer's New York World Building (briefly the tallest building in the world) as well as the original New York Times building

The facades are constructed from cast stone. The upper four storeys are set back from the base with massive piers that accentuate the building's height. The sculptural scheme by Henry Kreis features six groups of allegorical figures representing music, art, commerce and industry. The main entrance is flanked by 'Comedy and Tragedy on the left and 'Music and Art' on the right. 'Sport and Industry' are above the corner at 56th Street and 'Printing and the Sciences' are located on the corner at 57th Street